BUYING YOUR FIRST HORSE

A guide to happy horse ownership

WRITTEN AND ILLUSTRATED BY HEATHER LEDBETTER

For Papa

Your crazy love of horses inspired me. Rest in peace.

Table of Contents

PREFACE

I've lived most of my life under the influence of horses. My grandfather and great grandfather were both horsemen. They bred and showed Appaloosas in Washington state. Unfortunately, my grandfather passed away when I was only four years old, so I only got to share my love of horses with him briefly. There's so much I would have liked to talk with him about now that I have a deeper understanding of horses myself.

My real relationship with horses didn't begin until I was in my early twenties. I was a stay-at-home mother of one at the time and I needed to break away from that being my only purpose. I had grown up watching horse themed movies and they filled my head with a lot of wonderful, but very unrealistic views of how owning a horse would be. When I was working for my riding Instructor and friend, I was often charged with helping new riders with the basics of horsemanship. This was a task I really enjoyed because it was a chance to encourage others just like me in their journey. It was bittersweet to see the realization come to most of the students that working with horses was more difficult than they imagined.

I want to encourage people who dream about owning a horse the way I did that while working with and owning horses is far from easy, it can still be just as exciting and magical as you imagine it to be. You just need knowledge and a strong commitment to your animal.

As an equine massage instructor, I get to teach people how to help horses feel better from a physical standpoint. In this book I hope to teach you about helping your horse be happy in every aspect of their lives so that you can enjoy your relationship with them even more. I hope very much that you enjoy this book and what it has to offer.

THE BIG DECISION

Whether you've dreamed of owning a horse your whole life, or you are only recently contemplating the idea, you're probably aware that it's a pretty big decision to make.

There are many aspects of horse ownership to be considered before you can make an informed and confident decision. This book will address many of the most common questions that concern and perplex new owners.

The Time Factor:

Do you have the time for a horse?

This is a question you need to answer honestly. Horses require your time and energy to stay happy and healthy. If your horse will be staying on your property, you will need to feed and check their water each day, clear manure from their living space regularly, as well as groom and inspect them regularly to make sure they do not have any injuries. There's also the time that you will want to dedicate to training your horse if you have a desire to compete with them in any discipline.

If you opt to board your horse at a stable, depending on the type of boarding you are getting, you won't need to be there every day to care for them, but I still recommend that you be able to stop by the stable at least twice a week to see that your horse is being adequately cared for and that they are getting enough exercise. While the facility you choose will be taking your money in exchange for the care of your animal, you are still ultimately the one responsible for making sure they are doing well.

What if something happens and I don't have time for the horse anymore?

If there's one thing for certain in life, it's that life changes. Things come up and big life events take place that alter every aspect of our lives. When this happens, before you decide that you just don't have time for your horse and think about selling or rehoming it, consider a couple of options first. For example, you might find someone to do what's called a half or full lease of your horse while you settle back into a schedule that allows for more time. There are pros and cons to this option. Some of the pros being that you have someone paying your horse's expenses either in full or in part. That can take a lot of stress off of you if you run into a financial difficulty. Having someone lease your horse is also a good way to make sure that they still get exercise, even when you can't do that yourself. Some of the cons to leasing are that it can be difficult to find the right match for your horse. A badly matched lease can result in your horse reverting to bad habits or needing to re-train them under saddle in extreme cases. You may also run into issues with the person falling behind in payments, which can become an awkward situation.

Another possible solution is that you can loan your horse out to a riding program. If your horse is well behaved and good with most levels of riders, you can offer it to a riding school to use in their lesson program until you have time for the horse again. Research these programs in your area and contact a few stables to ask them if they are interested in taking on another lesson horse.

While these options aren't possible for everyone, they are a good alternative to selling your horse unnecessarily. Many people sell their horse and regret it and later down the road when they have time for them again.

The Money Factor:

Can I afford a horse?

This is probably the question that most people ask when it comes to buying a horse, and for good reason. Money matters. There's a lot of things that go along with this question, so I'm giving the subject its own chapter.

Buying VS. Adopting

Many people don't realize that there are lots of good horses available for adoption. Adopting a horse is typically much cheaper than buying and there is a wide variety of horses to choose from for any age or ability of rider. The downside to this is that if you adopt and decide the horse isn't a good fit for you after the typical trial period, you return the horse to the rescue (they don't allow you to sell it since they don't want it going back to auction) and you don't usually get your money back. This just means that you should really make sure that the horse is the right fit for you before deciding to adopt it. Besides that, adopting is a wonderful option since there are so many horses out there needing good homes.

HOW MUCH DOES A HORSE COST?

There's a saying that goes "There's no such thing as a free horse." That's a very true statement. Even if you were to get a horse for free, there are continuous costs associated when a horse. I'm going to break things down to give you an idea of both the upfront, and the on-going costs and their general price range.

Upfront	On-Going	Misc.
Purchase price/Adoption Fee: $-$$$$$$ Pre-purchase exam: $$$ Brand inspection: $$ Transporting horse: $$-$$$$	Farrier: $$-$$$ Preventative vet care: $$-$$$ Board (if your horse is not on your property): $$$-$$$$ Lessons/Training: $$-$$$	Emergency vet calls: $$$-? Tack: $$-$$$$$ Blankets: $$-$$$ Clinics: $$-$$$$ Showing: $$-?

This chart gives you just a general idea of how much a horse can cost. The cost will vary a little from year to year depending on you and your horse's needs. If you only do light riding on your horse and they don't need shoes, your costs will obviously be less than someone who's horse is in regular training and showing that needs to have a full set of shoes.

If you plan to keep your horse on your own property, the monthly expense might be a little less, but you still need to consider the cost of feed and water.

Upfront

-The purchase price/adoption fee for a horse will vary greatly. The average healthy, rideable, well-mannered horse will cost anywhere from $1,500 to upward of $10,000 for fancier riding horses. Show bred horses can cost twice that if not more depending on the horse's breeding, It's training and achievements. It is certainly possible to get a horse for less than the above-mentioned prices. Adoption is a great option for people with a lower budget (which I'll cover in another chapter).

-A <u>pre-purchase exam</u> is a full body health exam done by a vet prior to a horse being purchased/adopted. It is strongly advised to protect your potential investment and make sure that the horse you want is capable and healthy enough to do the job you want it to do. For example, if you want to compete in upper level jumping, a 20+ year old quarter horse isn't going to be the best fit for you.

-A <u>brand inspection</u> is mandatory and is required as proof of ownership. The inspection is conducted by an agent of the Department of Agriculture in your state (in the U.S.).

-Not everyone owns a trailer, so <u>transporting your horse</u> may be another expense to consider.

On-Going

-A good <u>farrier</u> is a must in your horse's on-going healthcare. There's a saying that goes "No hoof. No horse." And it's extremely true. So much of the horse's health comes from the hooves being well balanced and maintained on a regular basis. The average horse should see the farrier every 6 to 8 weeks depending on their needs.

-<u>Preventative vet care</u> is also a must when it comes to your horse's health. Regular dental checks and parasite prevention will help to keep your horse from getting sick and having problems.

-<u>Board</u> costs will vary greatly depending on the type of care that's being given and your location. Some stables offer self-care where you pay less each month, but you have to feed, water, and clean up after your horse. Other facilities offer full-care which means you just need to go out to groom and ride your horse, but these are typically much more expensive.

-Some horses need to be in regular <u>training</u> to be ready for competition, which can cost a good deal depending on the trainer's rates. You as the owner may also want to take riding <u>lessons</u> to improve your chances of winning at shows if that is part of your plan.

Misc.

-As much as we all wish we could avoid them, <u>emergency vet calls</u> happen. Horses can be prone to accidents and illness and there's just no avoiding an unplanned vet visit. One way to avoid accidental injuries is to check your horse's living space regularly for things that might cut or scratch them, or that the horse could become tangled in.

-Every horse owner usually ends up buying some miscellaneous items from time to time like new <u>tack</u> (saddles, bridles, pads, boots, etc.), as well as things like winter <u>blankets</u> and fly sheets. There's always something to buy for the barn.

-<u>Clinics</u> are a great way to expose your horse to a variety of different things. Top clinicians and professional horsemen all over the world offer clinics that allow riders and their horses to learn new and valuable things from the best of the best. Clinics will vary greatly in price depending on the caliber and popularity of the person teaching it. This is a great opportunity to grow as a horseman/woman and help your horse improve in their discipline or fix problems they might be having.

-<u>Showing</u> can be a fun and rewarding activity for you and your horse. Just keep in mind that there are many costs associated with getting to a horse show that include show clothes, show tack, special grooming supplies, class entry fees, haul-in and stall fees, etc. It can all add up very quickly. If you want to show without the price tag, you can research local riding clubs that have horse shows once a month and cost just a fraction of the price to enter. Typical prizes given at these shows are ribbons, small trophies, and occasionally small cash prizes.

Other expenses that you might want to consider are a vehicle for hauling and a horse trailer. This might not be a necessity for everyone, but having your own trailer can save your horse's life in the event of an evacuation of your area due to fire, flooding, etc. It also allows you to venture out with your horse and get to a show without having to pay someone else to haul your horse.

BREEDS OF HORSE

Once you've established that you are ready to start looking for a horse, there's usually the questions of what breed to look for. While there are many wonderful breeds and cross-breeds out there to choose from, you should consider what your riding discipline of choice is. First, we'll discuss the different riding disciplines.

- DRESSAGE: Dressage is a form of riding on the flat that requires horse and rider to work together to perform some very technical movements with the utmost accuracy and grace.
- JUMPERS: Show jumping is a speed event where horse and rider must successfully complete a course of jumps without making mistakes like knocking down rails or taking jumps out of order.
- HUNTERS: Hunters are a class of competitor that also jump a course of fences, but they are required to do so in a more controlled and relaxed manner, still making sure not to knock down polls or take jumps out of order.
- CROSS-COUNTRY: This is a very fast paced, endurance testing event where horse and rider must jump a variety of fences and objects over a long, typically outdoor field.
- ENDURANCE: Endurance is exactly what it sounds like. It is a race where horse and rider must trek across many miles of terrain to arrive at the finish line first.
- REINING: An event where horse and rider must complete a specific pattern with accuracy and style. The pattern includes circles, spins and sliding stops.
- CUTTING: This fast-paced event is designed to show off the abilities of the horse and rider to single out and move a cow from a herd without the cow getting away before the time is up.
- ROPING: Horse has to quickly follow a cow so that the rider can rope it, jump off the horse and tie the cow's feet together in the fastest time. Team roping is the same accept one team member tries to rope the cow by the head and the other tries to rope it by a back foot.
- PLEASURE: English and Western Pleasure classes are similar accept for the tack and attire of the rider. The horse and rider are judged on things like how relaxed they are, as well as the horse's ability to move in a consistently smooth way

throughout any gait. Each judge looks for different things, but that is typically what they look for.

- HALTER: This is a class that is done in-hand rather than under saddle. The horse and handler must complete a pattern and are judged on appearance, the horse's way of moving, as well as how the horse and handler move and stop together. Horses that are too young to be ridden are often shown in halter classes.
- POLO: Polo is another very fast-paced event where teams of riders try to score points by hitting a ball into a goal from horseback.
- GYMKHANA: This is a series of speed events such as pole bending, barrel racing, and key hole. Horse and rider try to accurately complete a pattern in the fastest amount of time.

Now that you are familiar with the different disciplines, let's talk about some of the different breeds of horse.

- ARABIAN: Known for their refined facial features, petite frame and desert roaming heritage, Arabian horses are commonly used for endurance events, trail riding, and pleasure.
- THOROUGHBRED: One of the most famous horse breeds due to the horse racing industry, the thoroughbred is typically a tall, refined horse with lots of energy. They are used most often for racing, jumping and pleasure.
- WARMBLOODS These heavier built sport horses have grace, power and beauty. They are most commonly used for dressage, jumping, and pleasure.
- QUARTER HORSE: These symbols of the American west are sturdy, athletic horses that are commonly used in cattle work, halter classes, gymkhana, and pleasure.
- FRESIAN: Known for their stunning black coat and long flowing mane and tail, the Fresian horse is a beautiful mover and used often for dressage, driving and pleasure.
- MUSTANG: These horses are hardy, athletic and resilient. They typically excel at things like cutting, speed events, and trail riding, but are also a very versatile breed.
- MORGAN: These compact and graceful horses are commonly used for trail riding, cutting, jumping, pleasure, and driving.
- DRAFT BREEDS: These are the heavyweights of the horse world. Breeds such as the Clydesdale, Percheron, Belgians and Shires are often used for driving and hauling heavy loads. They are also reliable trail and pleasure horses.
- SADDLEBRED: These horses are commonly found in the show ring. They are typically a gaited breed and are known for their style and strong presence.

Though typically used for saddle-seat competitions, they can be used for a variety of things such as pleasure, driving, jumping and endurance.

- TENNESSEE WALKING HORSE: Another gaited breed, the TWH is known for being a flashy mover with a calm disposition. They are commonly used for trail riding, pleasure, saddle-seat, and endurance.
- ROCKY MOUNTAIN HORSE: Typically gaited, the RMH is best known for their chocolate colored coat with a flaxen mane and tail. These horses are commonly used for trail riding, working cattle, and pleasure.

This is just a small list of the many breeds in the world. Do your research and choose a breed that excels at your chosen discipline. Most breeds can be great trail horses with enough miles and experience.

BASIC HORSE ANATOMY TERMS

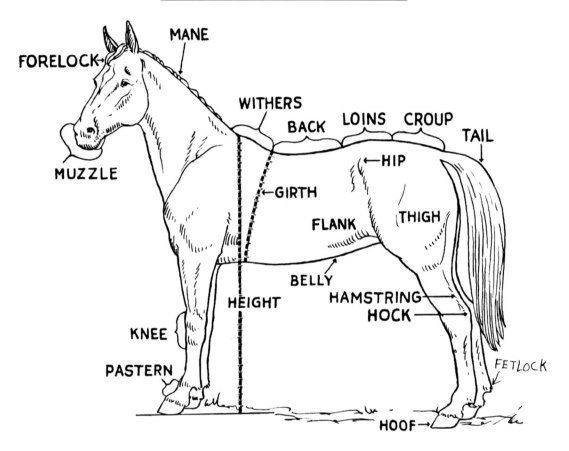

Knowing basic horse anatomy is important because it helps you be able to better communicate with your vet and other equestrians when it comes to your horse's health and training.

In addition to the diagram above, the boney bump at the top of the horse's head between the ears is referred to as the poll, and the horse's "knee" is referred to as the stifle.

UNDERSTANDING HORSE BEHAVIOR

Horses are flight or "prey" animals and they have very definite body language that is basically universal throughout the equine family. By studying their behavior over the years, people have learned a lot about what much of the behavior means. Below are some examples.

BEHAVIOR	TYPICAL REASON
Pinning ears back	Usually done when a horse is irritated or giving a warning. Horses also do this when running at top speeds.
Bucking	Done in play, during fights, response to pain or resistance to work
Rearing	Not unlike bucking, rearing is done in most cases of play, during fights, as a fear response, or resistance to work
Raising upper lip	Known as the Flehmen response, this is usually done to enhance sense of smell
Cribbing, or "wind sucking"	Often this is done out of stress or boredom. The action of pressing their teeth on a hard surface and sucking in air creates an endorphin release, which is why this behavior can be difficult to stop.
Licking and chewing	This is a result of the nervous system shifting gears. The licking and chewing response is brought on by the "let-down" of salivation, usually after the horse has been in a situation of stress (altercation in the herd) or concentration (like when in training)
Vocalizations like the "whinny"	Usually done when the horse is stressed, excited, anticipating food, or when the horse is trying to communicate with herd members from a distance. Horses also often "squeal" at each other as a warning.

SUPPLIES

Every owner needs to stock up on supplies for their new horse. This list is helpful for preparing people who are going to keep a horse on their own property. It is also for those who have to board their horse because it gives them an idea of what a boarding facility should have.

BARN		TACK ROOM	
Muck rake	Bucket for manure	blankets	Saddle racks
Hay feeders (ground level)	Water trough/buckets	Fly sheet/fly mask	Hooks for bridles
Dry storage for hay	Shelter for horse to get out of bad weather/sun	Halters and lead ropes	Grooming kit (hoof pick, curry comb, brushes)
Paddock or turnout	Round pen	Fly spray	Supplements
Crossties or hitching post	Grain storage	Saddle pads	Saddle
Water access	Strong, safe fencing	Bridle	Boots/wraps
Wash rack	Rodent control	Helmet	Chaps
Wheel barrow	Fly control	Gloves	Bath supplies (shampoo, sponge, etc.)

Take time to think about what you might want to have in your barn/at a barn you would want to board at. Do you want it to have an indoor arena for year-round riding? Do you want your horse to have a paddock? Do you want a heated barn? Make yourself a list of supplies and amenities that you want for your horse to help you prepare.

HORSE NUTRITION

Knowing how to feed your new horse can seem daunting. There's a lot to know, right? Technically yes, there are people who have degrees in equine nutrition, but you don't have to know that much! Here are some simple rules to follow when it comes to your horse's nutrition.

-Horses are designed to eat a diet of mostly forage, so quality hay is a must in their diet. The average thousand-pound horse needs about fifteen to twenty pounds of hay per day.

-The horse's digestive system works better when there is a steady flow of feed going through it. For this reason, it is best to feed your horse little and often, versus meal feeding a couple of times per day. Hay pillows can help to prevent the horse from eating their food too fast.

-Horses are designed to eat with their head low to the ground. It makes for a healthy back, and a healthy respiratory system, so make sure your horse is eating low to the ground whenever possible.

-Constant access to clean water is a must.

-Grain is usually only needed to supplement good quality hay if extra calories are needed for performance or weight gain. When trying to increase calorie intake, consider a higher fat feed rather than a higher sugar feed to avoid the horse becoming "hot".

-It's recommended that the horse has access to a mineral or salt block. This will help the horse get minerals that it needs and encourage more water consumption.

-Alfalfa is a good source of calcium for the horse and can help prevent ulcers, but it's usually only recommended that you mix a small amount of alfalfa in with your regular hay if you choose to feed it. Feeding your horse straight alfalfa or large amounts of it is usually not recommended as it can have some negative side effects. It's a good idea to consult your vet when considering adding alfalfa to your horse's diet.

UNDERSTANDING TACK

There are many different styles of tack from all around the world to choose from, but this just covers the two most common types of saddle and bridle.

SADDLES

English   Western

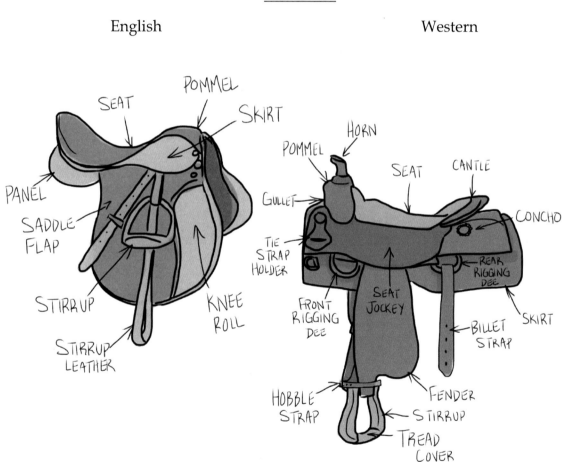

The part of the saddle that goes around the horse's belly and attaches to the billet straps under the saddle flap or fender is referred to as the girth for English saddles and the cinch for Western saddles.

BRIDLES

English   Western

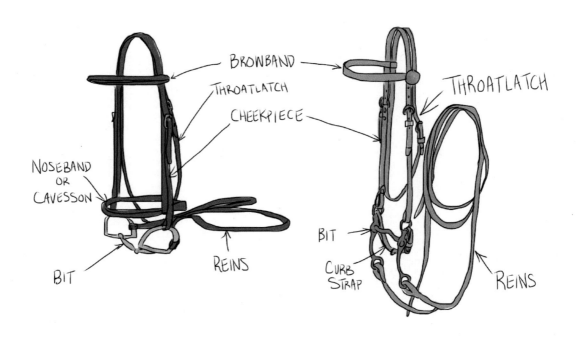

There are other pieces of equipment that can be added to bridles and saddles for training purposes, such as the martingale or "tie down". This is a device used for keeping the horse from raising their head too high in certain disciplines, or to simply teach the horse to keep their head in a lower position when being ridden. There are two common forms of the martingale, the "running" martingale which attaches to the girth and then splits into two leather straps that attach to each side of the reins. This allows for more movement. The other is the "standing" martingale. This is usually a single leather strap that goes from the girth to the underside of the noseband and is usually more restrictive for the horse. Another common piece of equipment used on a saddle would be the breast collar, which is used to add stability to the saddle when the horse is in work that requires sudden movements (cutting), or steep uphill or downhill work (trail riding). The breast collar goes around the front of the horse on the chest and attaches to the girth and on either side of the saddle on d-rings. It creates a Y shape that keeps the saddle from rotating or sliding back on the horse.

BRINGING YOUR HORSE HOME

Bringing home your new horse is a very exciting time. You'll want to make sure that you have everything ready to go before your horse arrives.

-If you are boarding your horse, make sure that the owner of the facility is aware of your horse's arrival day and time and has given you instructions on where the horse will need to go when it arrives.

-Make sure that if you are keeping your horse in a place with other horses, you separate the new horse from the others for at least ten days. This prevents the spread of illness and allows the horses to get used to each other's presence before they can be allowed to come in any sort of contact with each other.

-Request that the previous owner provides you with a few days-worth of feed for the horse so that you can introduce the new feed slowly. Change in feed should always be done slowly to avoid digestive upset.

-You'll want to make sure that your horse is eating, drinking, and passing manure well in the days following their arrival. Travel can be very stressful on horses and they can be prone to colic as a result.

-Remember that moving is a big event for a horse. They can take weeks and even a few months to acclimate fully to their new surroundings. The best thing you can do for your horse is get it into a regular work routine as soon as possible to prevent it from getting bored or anxious in their new surroundings. Work is good for the horse's brain and morale. Once a horse is in a consistent work routine and has a chance to bond with their owner as well as other horses or animals that it lives with, they will usually settle in nicely.

BUILDING YOUR RELATIONSHIP:

There are lots of ways to build a relationship with your horse. Grooming, riding, and just being with your horse can help boost their connection with you. However, one of the best ways to build a trusting relationship is through groundwork.

What is groundwork? Groundwork is training done from off the horse's back. This work can be done anywhere, though I have found that a round pen is a fantastic place to work on this because it allows space enough for you to work, while keeping the horse in a safe place where if it accidently got away from you, it wouldn't run off.

What does groundwork accomplish? Horses are herd animals. Even though they are away from a herd, they are still looking for leadership and guidance. To communicate in the herd, a horse will often move the feet of another horse to establish themselves as a leader in the group. In a similar way, we create movement in the horse's feet by asking them to lunge around us (either on a line or freely in a round pen), back up, and yield the front or hind end to us. This establishes you as a source of guidance for the horse and you will see how quickly the horse begins to look for that guidance.

What tools do you need to do groundwork? The most important thing is a good, solid halter and lead rope. A sturdy rope halter with a long lead (at least 15 feet long) is usually best. You may also opt to have a carrot stick to extend your touch and as a safety precaution if your horse is a bit on the "hot" side.

What exercises do you do during groundwork? This will depend on what you are trying to accomplish in your horse's training, but in general we teach the horse to lunge around us on the lead in a relaxed and controlled manner. This takes time with some horses, but it is valuable for bringing the horse's mind back to you when they get nervous in any situation. You can work on changing directions frequently to keep the horse's attention on you. Asking the horse to back up, flexing their neck to both sides, and yielding the forehand and hind are all ways to work with the horse from the ground. You can teach them lots of things this way that can translate to the saddle.

HOOKING ON

"Hooking on" is what most people call the moment when a horse decides to come to you and follow you without the aid of a lead being attached to them. This can be accomplished with pretty much any horse.

When you free-lunge (work the horse around you in a round pen without using a lead rope or lunge line), you will ask the horse to move away from you in either direction around the pen. Often the first time you do this exercise, the horse will not be sure what to do, so you just keep after them to move away from you (You can use your lead rope, lunge whip or carrot stick to encourage them to move if the horse is feeling lazy). Once they start to move freely around you, you can make them switch directions by carefully moving in front of the horse so it is cut off and has to go the other way. Do not attempt to cut them off if they are galloping or seem frantic because the horse may run into you. First wait for them to slow down or relax before you ask them to change directions. It's best to encourage the horse to turn their head in towards you as it changes directions, rather than their butt. This will help keep you connected and prevent the horse from being able to kick out at you if they're feeling feisty. If the horse turns their butt to you anyway, ask it to change directions again until they stop giving you their butt. Always reward the horse's effort to give you what you want by taking some of the pressure off of them. Often this is as simple as lowering your eyes so they aren't looking directly into the horse's eyes. Once you've worked with the horse in each direction for a few minutes, start to look for signs that the horse is ready to stop (licking and chewing, lowering the head, looking in towards you). When you notice these signs, take the pressure completely off by not asking them to move away from you anymore and see if they will turn into you and move towards you. If the horse is apprehensive, turn away from the horse for a moment (while still being fully aware of where the horse is for your safety). Usually this is when the horse will ask to come into your space. You can reward them with rubs on the nose and neck (they usually like that). At this point you can try to walk away and see if they will follow you. If they walk off in a different direction, you can go back to your "sending away" exercise and try again. Some horses will hook onto you very quickly, others may take more time. This is something that you can do for exercise, as well as to continue to build a relationship with the horse on a regular basis.

WHEN TO CALL THE VET

One of the most concerning topics for new owners is knowing when to call the vet. Knowing what symptoms need the vet's attention and the things that you can take care of yourself will save you a lot of unnecessary vet bills and worry. If you are ever unsure of what to do when your horse is hurt, call the vet. Even if they don't think they need to come and look at the horse, they can give you advice on what to do.

CALL THE VET IF:	SHOULDN'T NEED TO CALL VET IF:
There is a deep or excessively bloody wound.	There is a small, clean looking wound that isn't bleeding much and isn't swollen or hot.
There is excessive swelling anywhere	The horse looks a little stiff, but loosens up after moving around for a bit
There is discharge coming from a wound	There are minor lumps and bumps on the horse that go away after a day or two.
The horse becomes uncoordinated	Horse's back legs are both equally a little swollen around the fetlock and pastern up to the hock. Movement and cold hosing should help reduce the swelling.
The horse is limping/non-weight bearing	Small circular sores on the fronts of the foreleg fetlocks. These are usually pressure sores that horses get from laying down and getting back up. You can use a pair of flexible rubber bell boots turned upside down on the front feet to prevent the sores on the fetlocks.
The horse is down and can't get back up	Horse has bite marks from another horse. These usually heal on their own.
The horse seems lethargic or uncomfortable	Horse has smelly, crumbly white stuff in the hoof (thrush). There are commercial products you can use to kill the bacteria.
The horse isn't eating, drinking, or passing manure.	There are small welts and bites on the horse from bugs. This is usually solved with increased bug protection like sheets, masks, boots and stronger fly spray.

COMMON PROBLEMS

Many owners struggle with a few common problems among horses. Here is a list of some of those problems and some common methods for correcting them.

PROBLEM

POSSIBLE SOLUTION

PROBLEM	POSSIBLE SOLUTION
Trailer loading-refusal to step onto the trailer.	Many people struggle with their horse refusing to load in the trailer. Groundwork is the first step to getting your horse on a trailer. Work with your horse on being able to send them through, between, and over things first. Once you can do that, approach the trailer and attempt to "send" the horse into the trailer. If the horse takes a step towards the trailer, reward that by letting the horse rest, then ask again. With each try, ask the horse to step into the trailer a little more. If the horse backs up and refuses to take a step into the trailer, go to work by lunging the horse, backing and other groundwork exercises. After a minute or two of that immediately try to send the horse into the trailer again. The horse will learn that they can rest in the trailer. Another solution is to back the trailer up to the horse's run or pen and feed the horse in the trailer for every meal till they are comfortable in it. This can have mixed results though.
Trailering- Horse is nervous in the trailer	One of the best ways to get your horse to relax in the trailer is by having them trailer with an older or more relaxed horse. They feed off of the other horse's energy and usually calm down. Having hay for the horse to eat is also good.

Horse bucks under saddle	This is a problem that a lot of people struggle with and it can become very dangerous if not addressed immediately. The first thing to look for when a horse starts to buck is any soreness in their body. Poor saddle fit can often result in the horse bucking to get rid of the discomfort it feels. Always try to rule out pain before you address a behavioral problem. If the horse is not in pain, you need to then look for things that may have caused the horse to spook if it bucks in a consistent spot. If a reason for the bucking can't be found otherwise, it's time to go back to the basics and do groundwork to find out if the horse is missing something important in their education.
Horse is mouthy/nippy	This often happens if the horse is hand fed treats. An easy solution to this is to feed treats to them in a feed bucket or cut out treats completely. If the horse is mouthy and does not get treats, the easiest solution is to discourage the behavior with a quick and firm pop to the pectoral area, side, or the side of the mouth. Mouthy horses can become horses that bite if it isn't corrected. Horses bite each other in play, so they aren't above biting a person if they think they're doing it in play.
Horse pushes you around on the ground	A horse that doesn't have a healthy respect for their handler will not respect that person's personal space. This can be very dangerous because if the horse spooks, they are more likely to push you over to get away from whatever scared them. Teaching the horse to keep at a safe distance from you when you are walking with them or standing still is very important for your safety. When you are walking with the horse, using the end of the lead rope, a crop, or a carrot stick,

	correct the horse by popping it on the chest when it gets too close to you. If you stop and the horse continues to walk forward, quickly and rapidly ask the horse to back up several steps. Rest for a moment so the horse can think and repeat the exercise until the horse understands to respect your personal space and not push past you when you've chosen to stop. You can do the backing exercise when standing still to get the horse to learn where the edge of your personal space is.
Horse is buddy or barn sour	Horses can easily become overly attached to another horse or the barn. When this happens, it makes it very difficult for the rider. The best method of dealing with this is to make the horse work in the place or with the horse that it doesn't want to leave. By making the horse work hard near the horse it doesn't want to be away from or in the barn that it wants to stay in, and then letting the horse rest away from those things helps the horse make the connection that it's harder to stay with than it is to leave those things.
Horse gets nervous in new places	This is a problem that will usually become easier as the horse builds their relationship with you because it will begin to look to you for confidence. In the mean-time though the best thing to do for a horse that's upset or nervous in a new place is to put the horse to work using their brain right away so it doesn't have the chance to react to the new surroundings. This is another place where groundwork comes in handy, as well as good exercises to put the horse to work at under saddle. The worst thing you can do when a horse is nervous is to let the horse stand around doing nothing.

THE REST IS UP TO YOU

Now that you have a guide to the basics of happy horse ownership, I hope that you'll continue to grow in your knowledge and experience. Get your butt in the saddle or in the cart, or on the ground with your horse and work towards your goals. With love, hard work and encouragement, your horse will take you anywhere you want to go.

Consistency is key in horsemanship and it's the key to your horse's potential. Be patient with your horse and more importantly be patient with yourself. If you're new to working with horses, you've got a long and wonderful journey ahead of you. Remember that no time spent with your horse is wasted time and make every encounter with them as positive as you can. If you can do that, you'll be on your way to happy horse ownership.

Cheers and happy trails!

ABOUT THE AUTHOR (AND HER HORSE)

Heather Ledbetter is a professional equine massage therapist and Instructor in beautiful Colorado. She has worked with many professionals in the horse world over the years to grow her knowledge of equine behavior and care. This is the first book she has written about horse ownership. She hopes to expand her love of writing and illustrating in the future with more books about horses.

Heather is a happy wife and the mother of two boys. When she isn't spending time with family or working, she enjoys working with her own horse, Kindle. Kindle was bound for slaughter, but she was rescued by Front Range Equine Rescue. She was in poor health and did not trust people. Kindle has come a long way since her rescue and now she and Heather enjoy riding the trails of Colorado and participating in local riding club events.

Made in the USA
Columbia, SC
18 June 2020

11588067R00015